Ladies In White

Hot Girls Sexy White Lingerie

By **EROTICA PHOTO ART LOVER**

Copyright © Ladies In White

All rights reserved. No part of this document may be
Reproduced or transmitted in any form or by any means, electronic, mechanical, photocopying,
Recording, or otherwise, without prior written permission of erotica photo art lover.

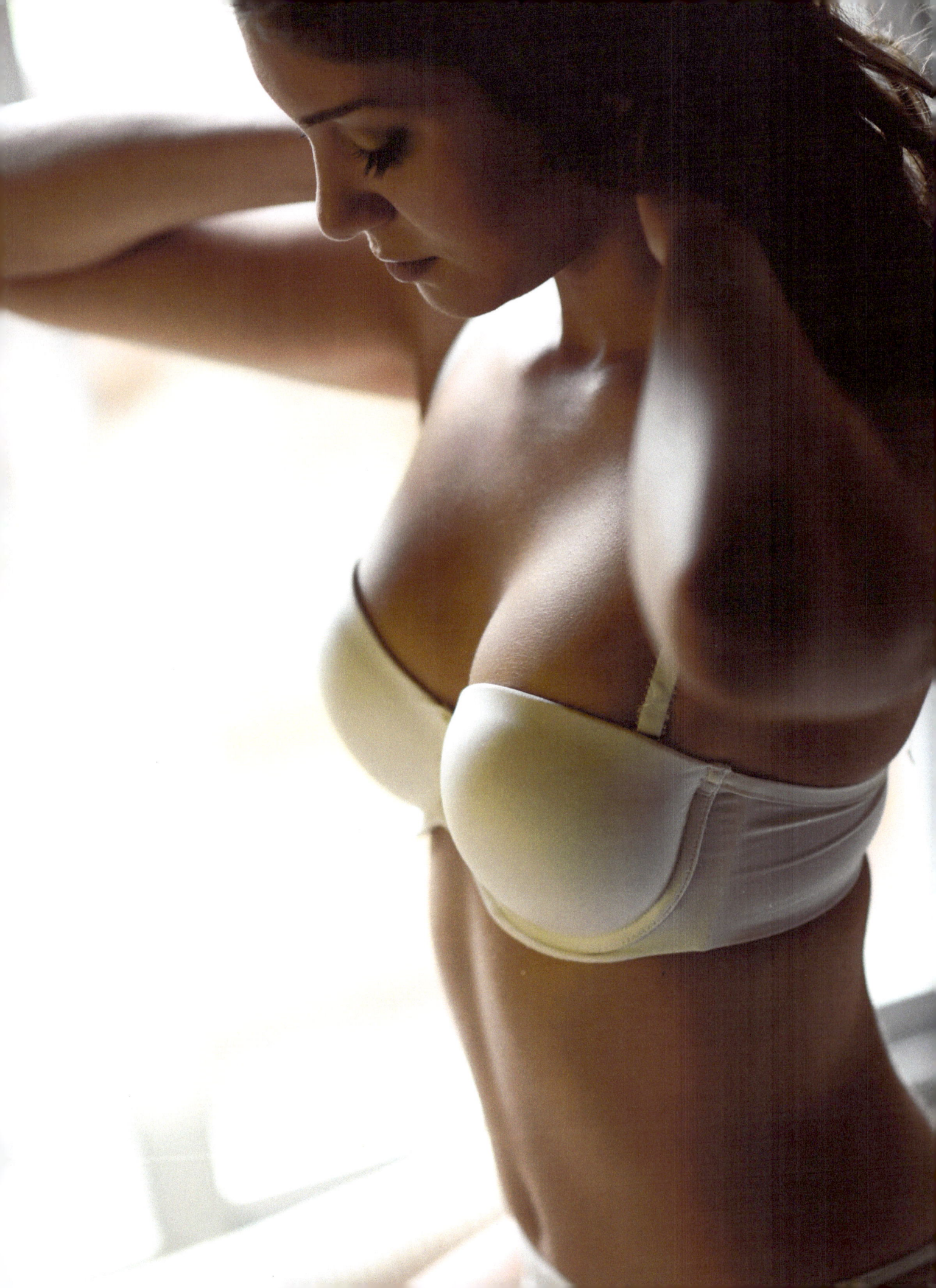

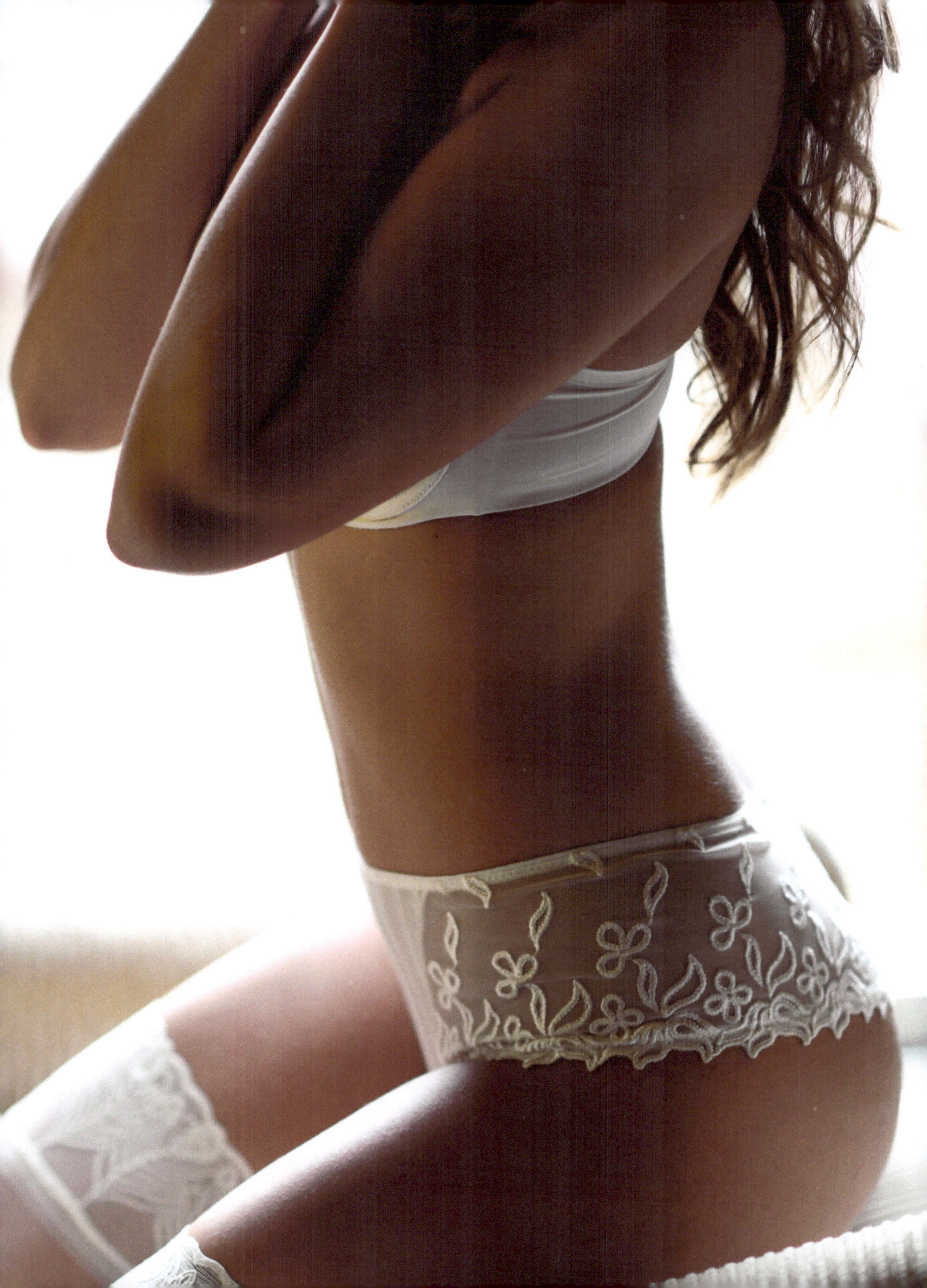

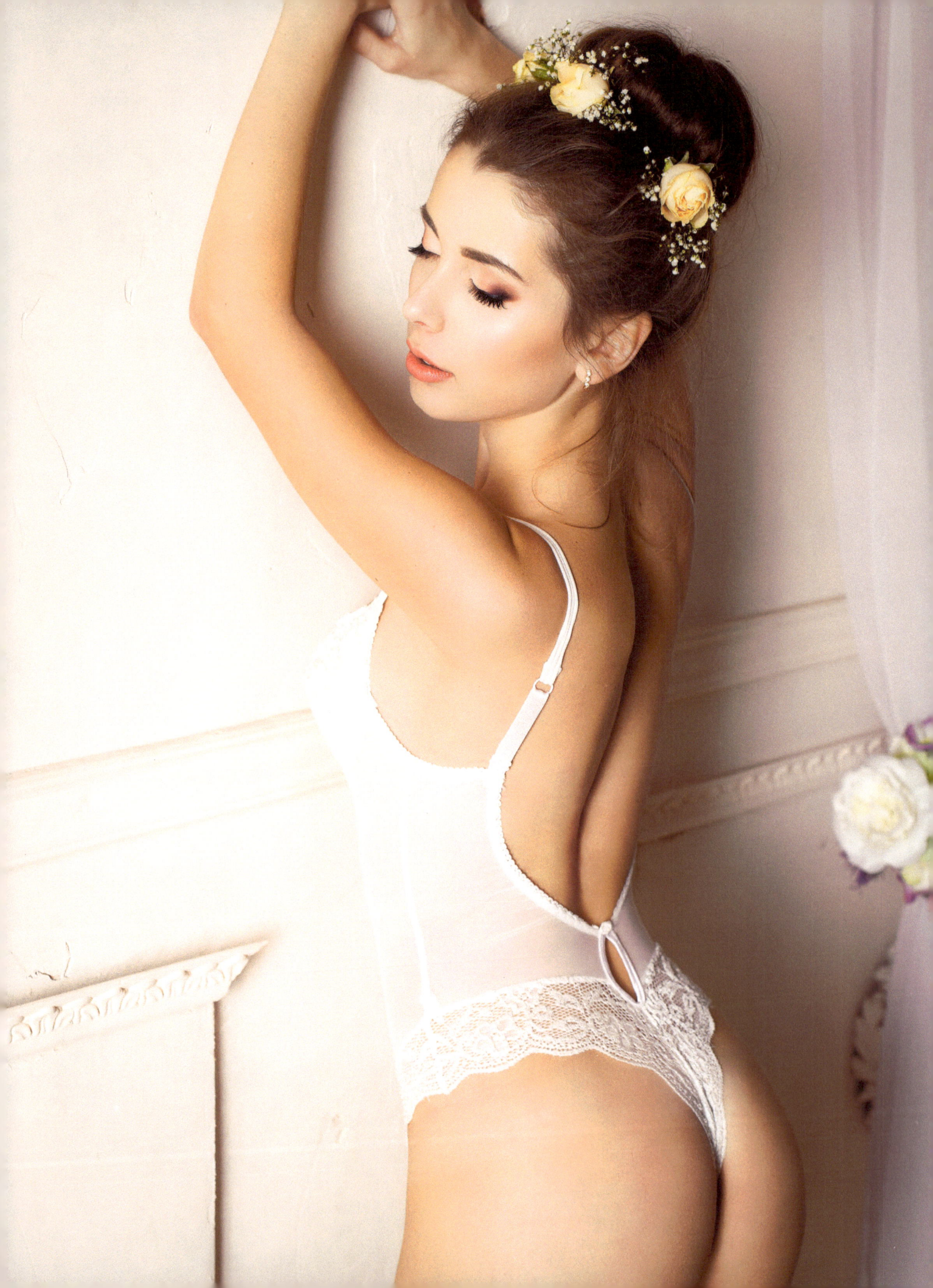

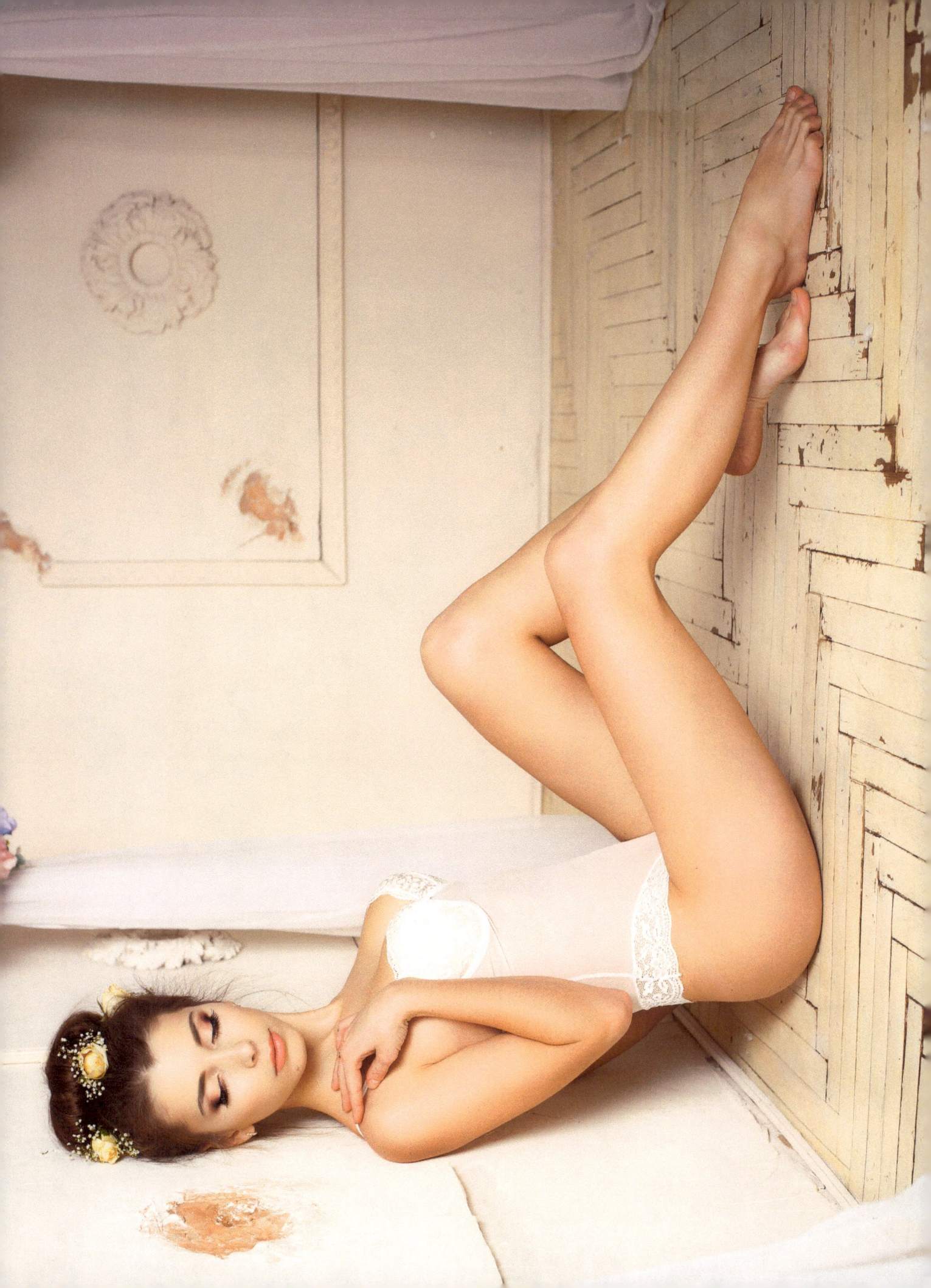

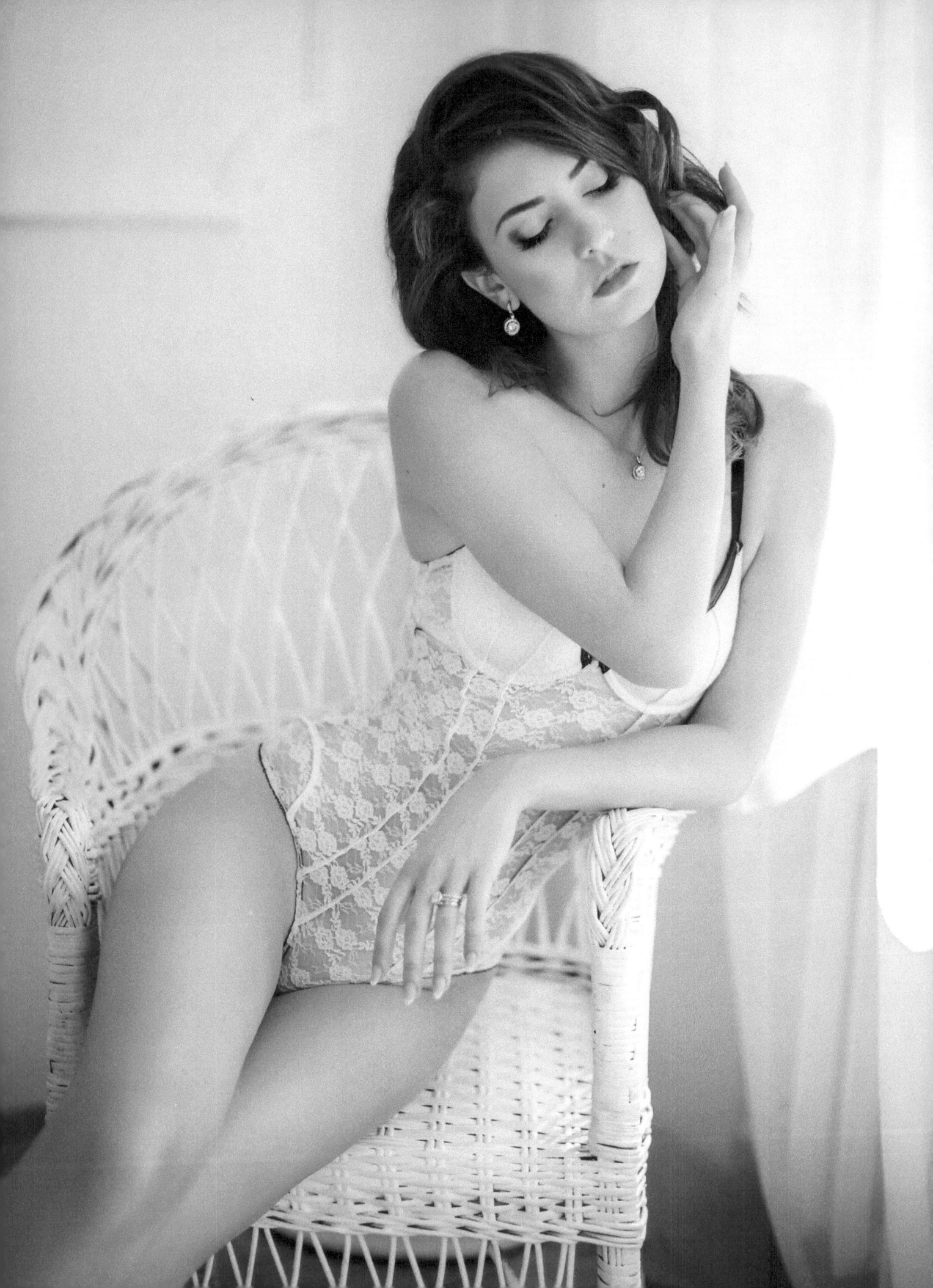

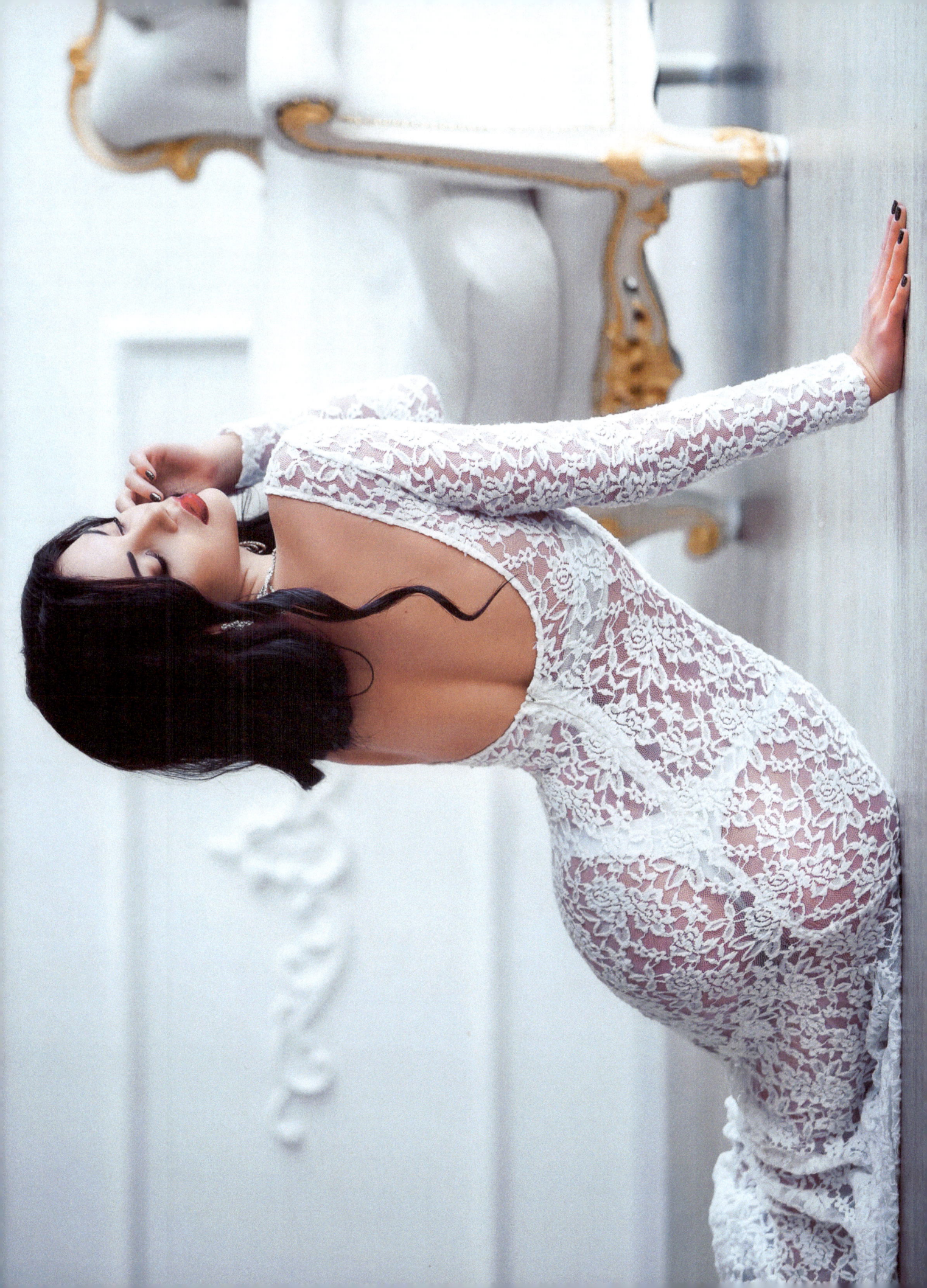

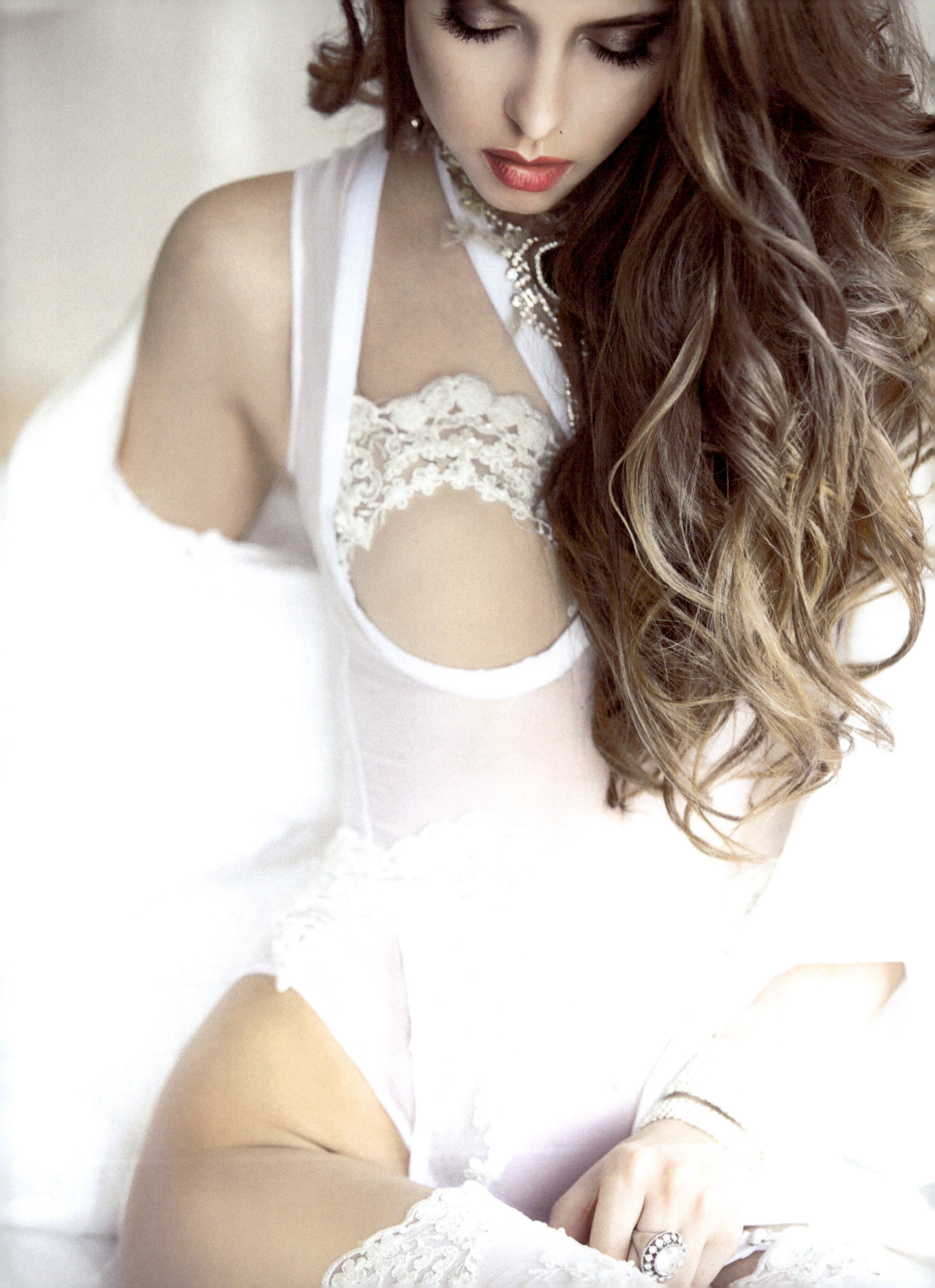

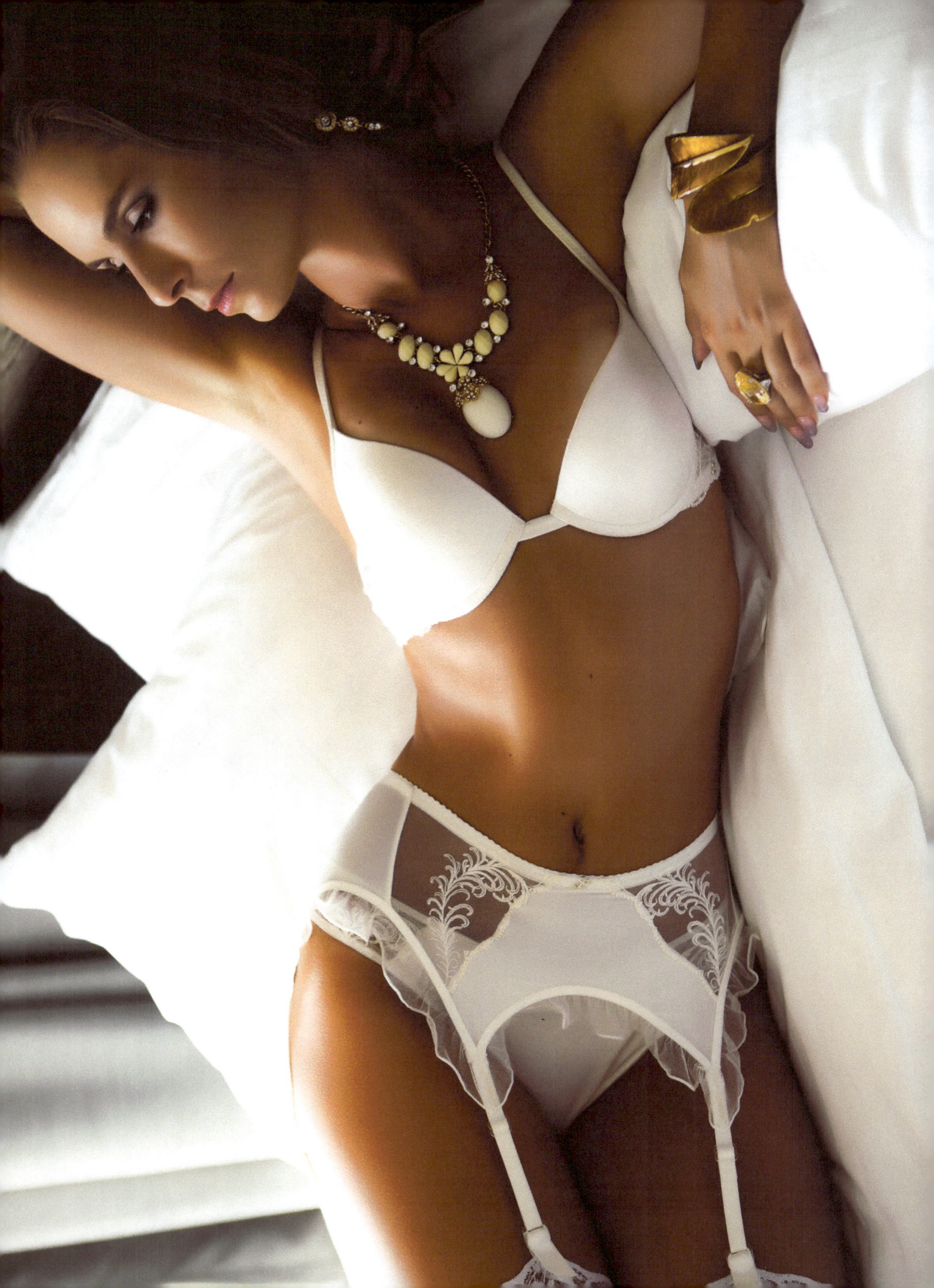

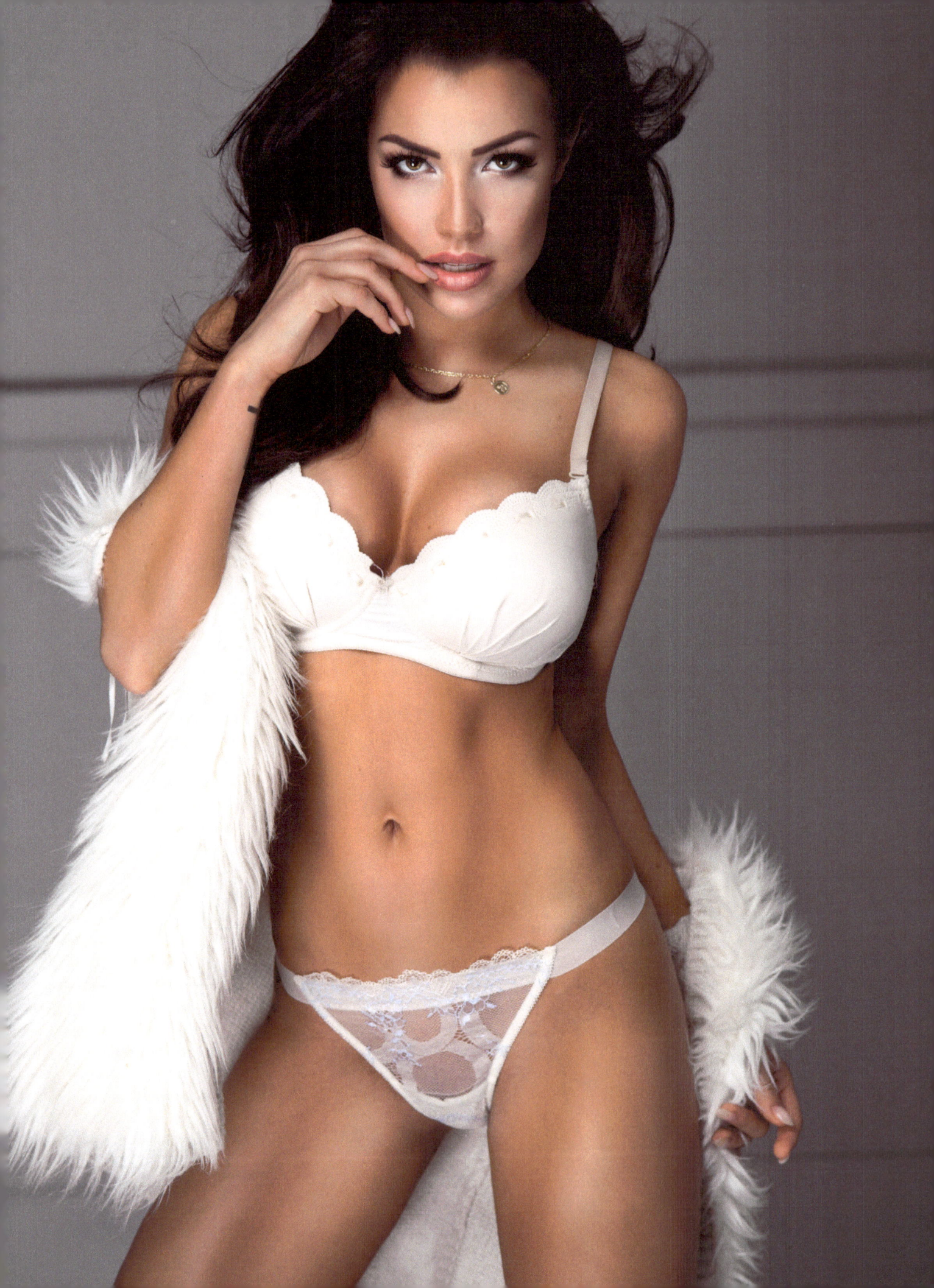

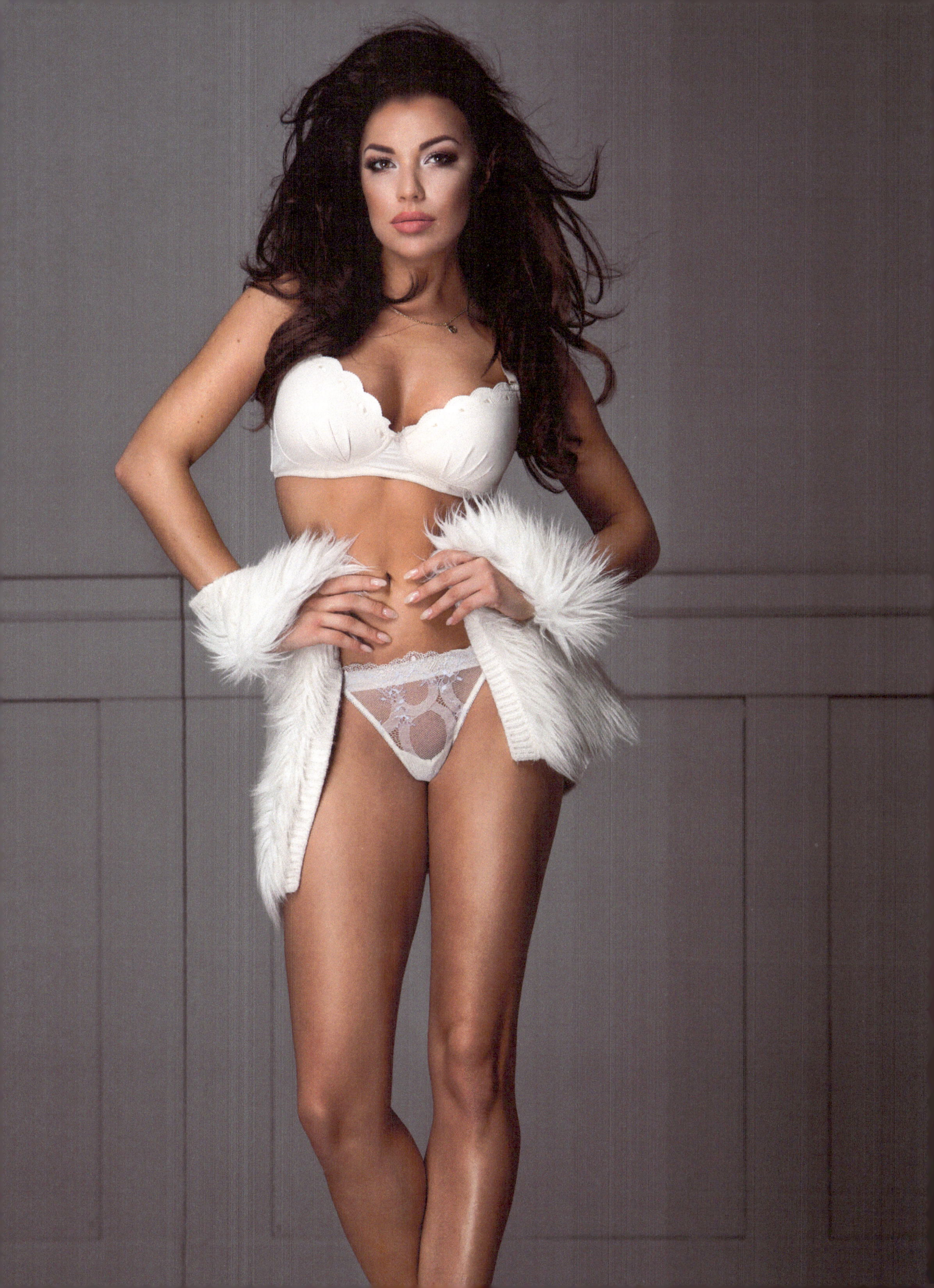

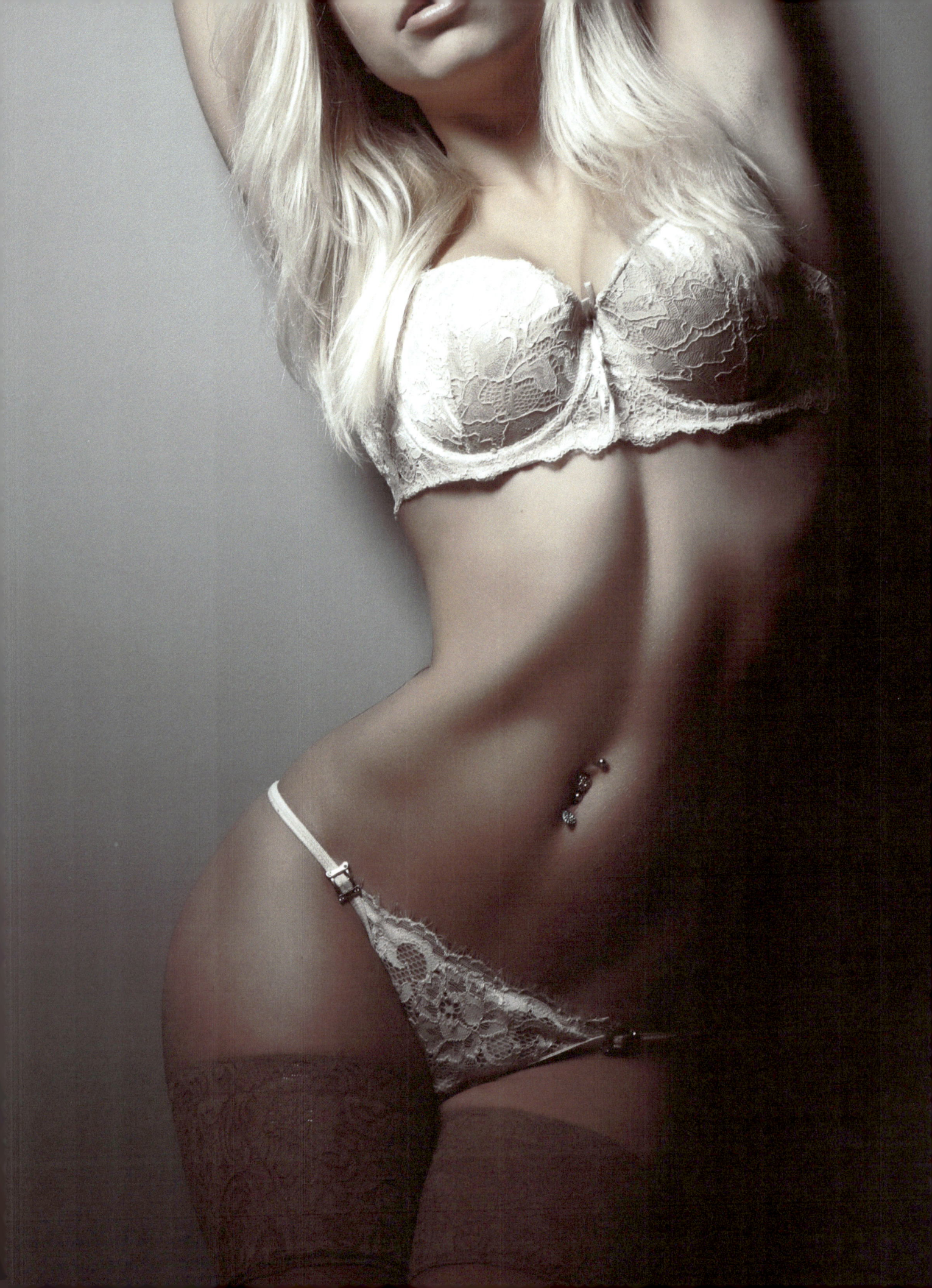

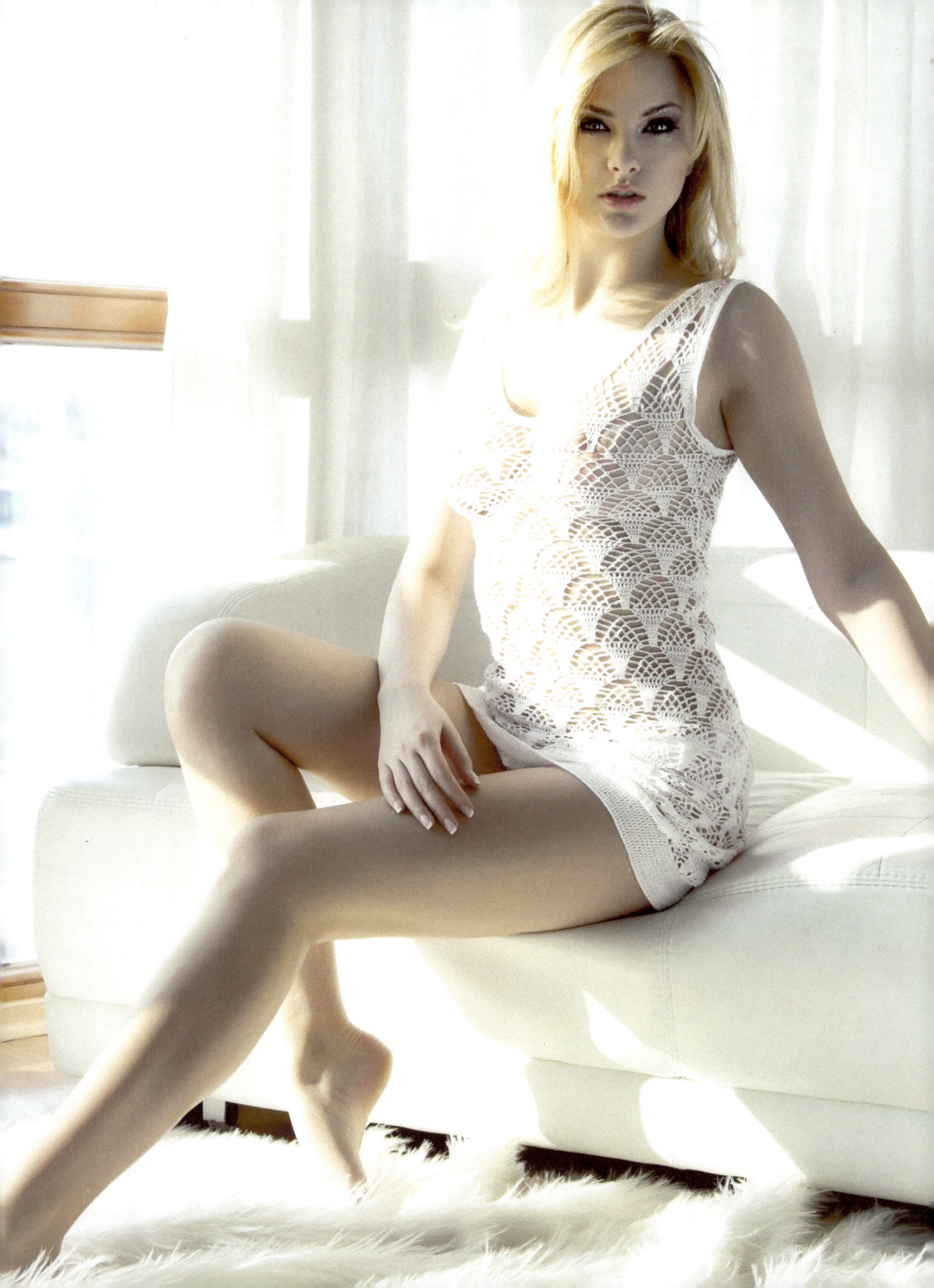

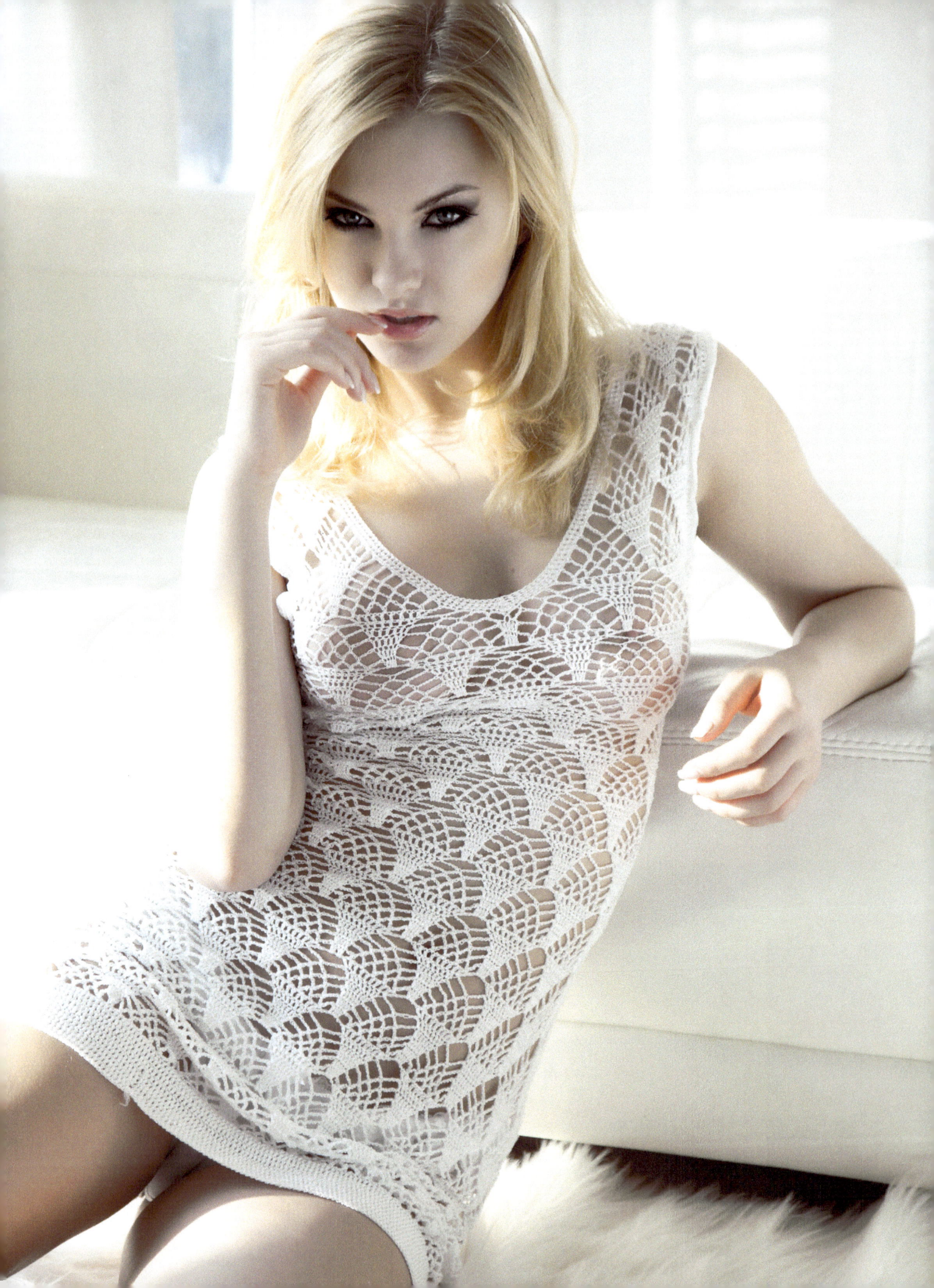

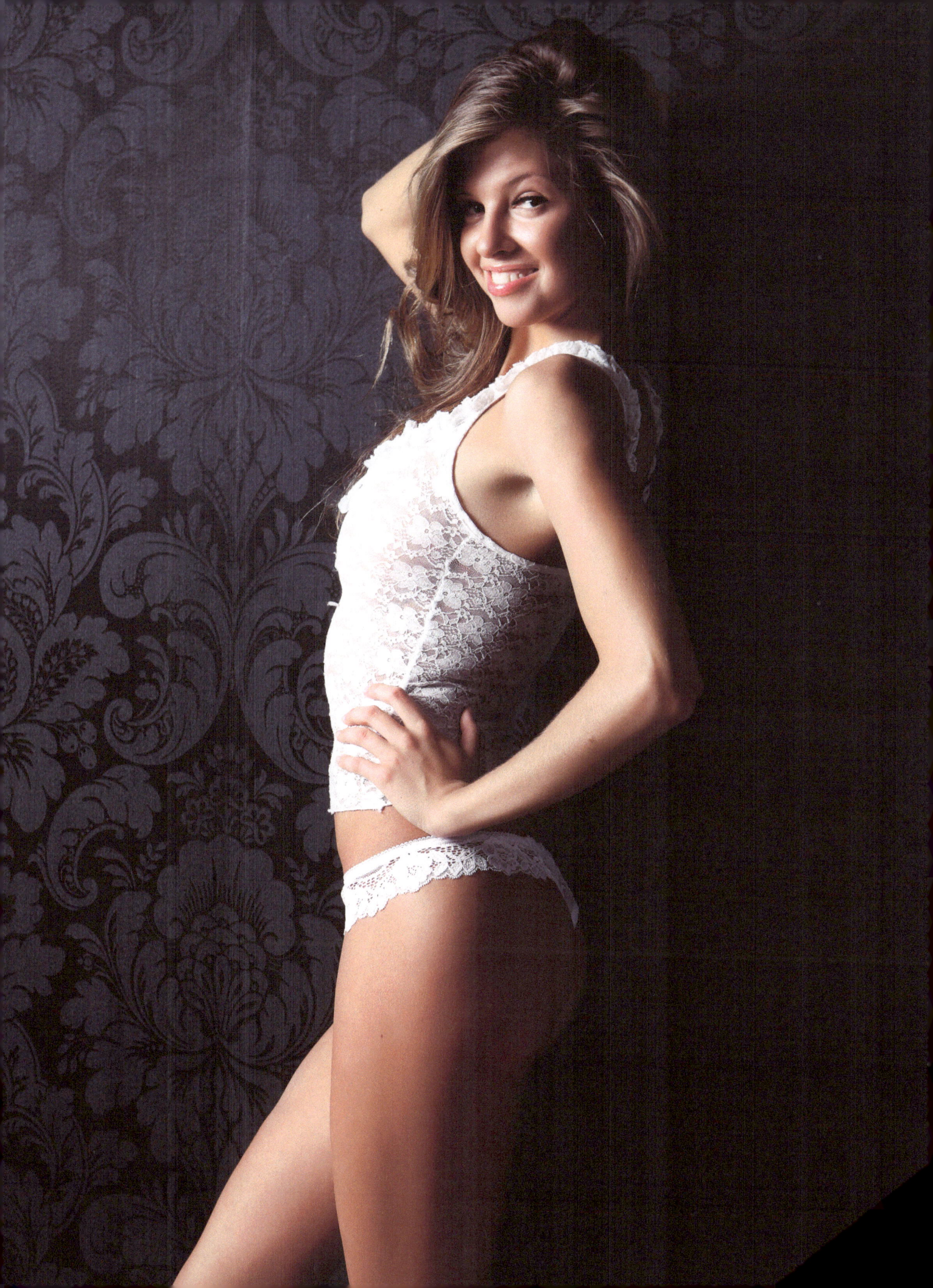

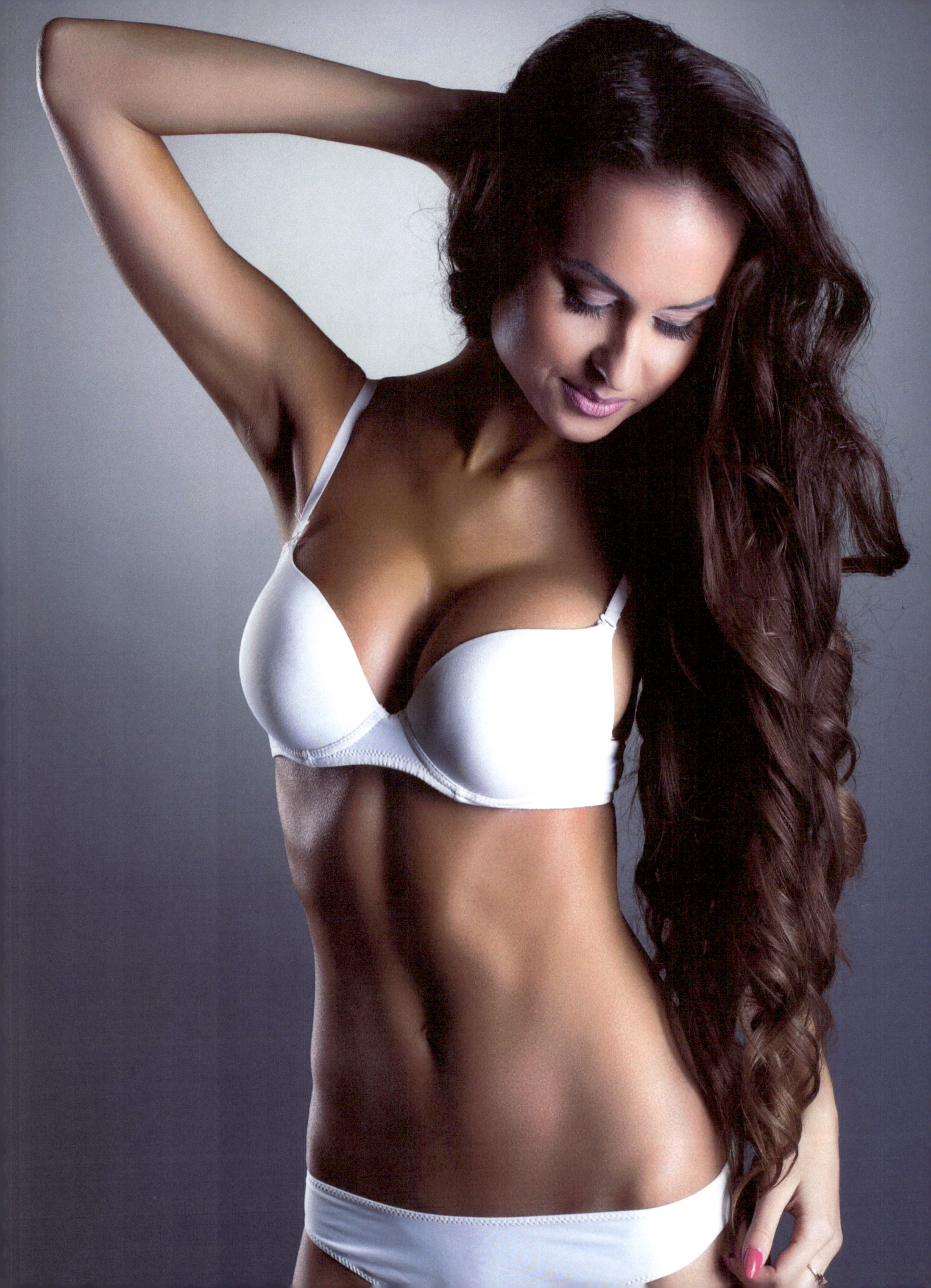

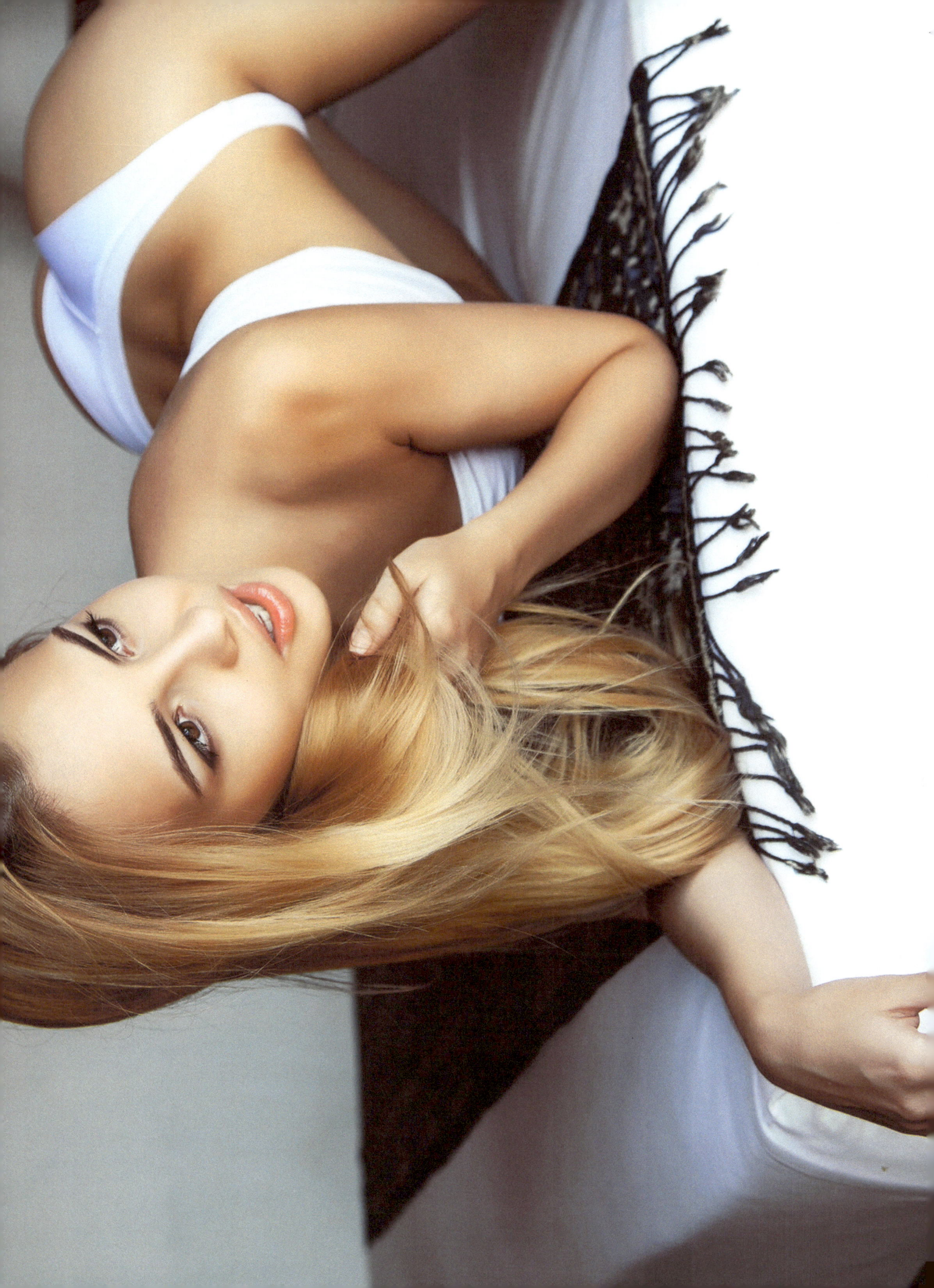

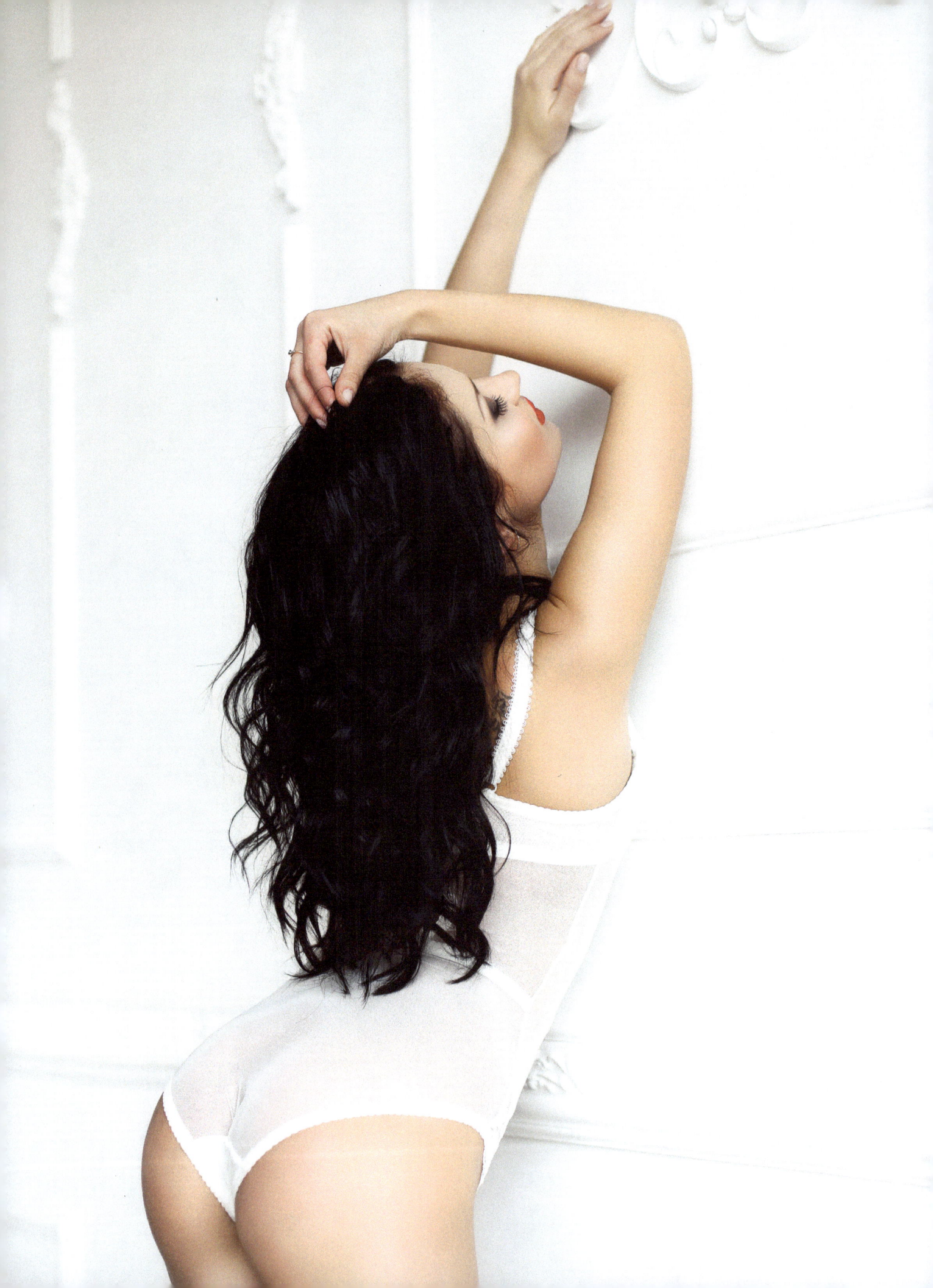

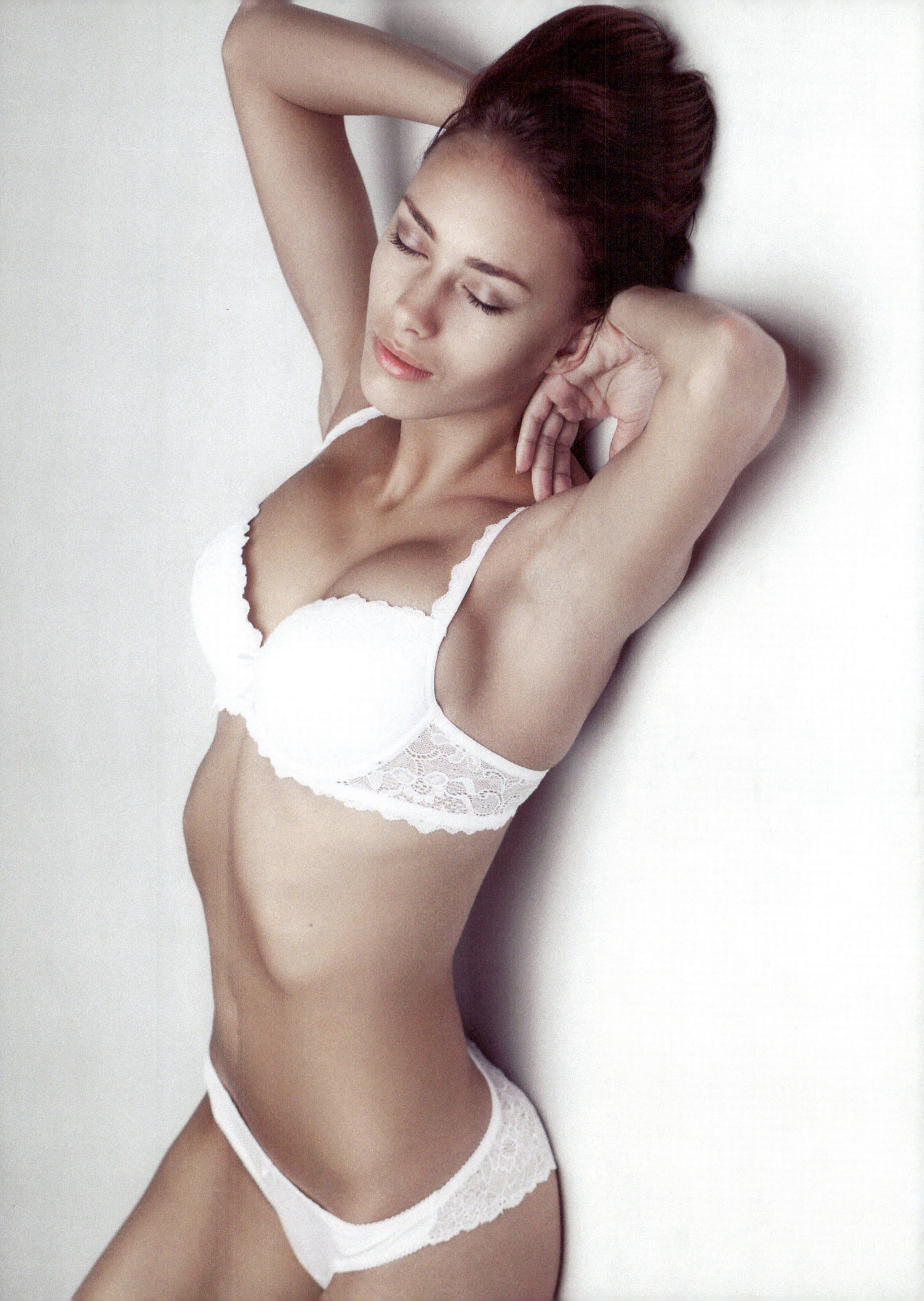

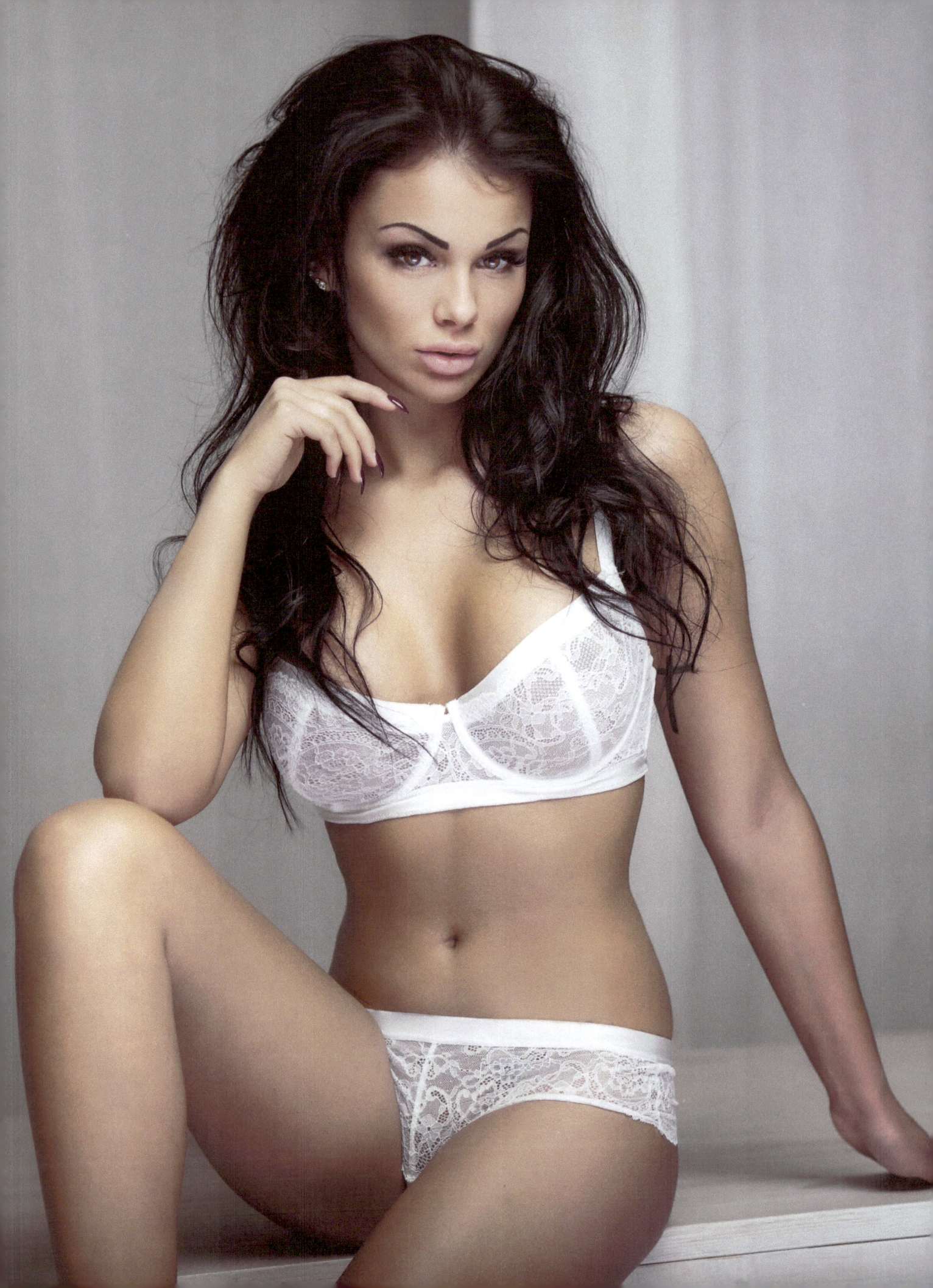

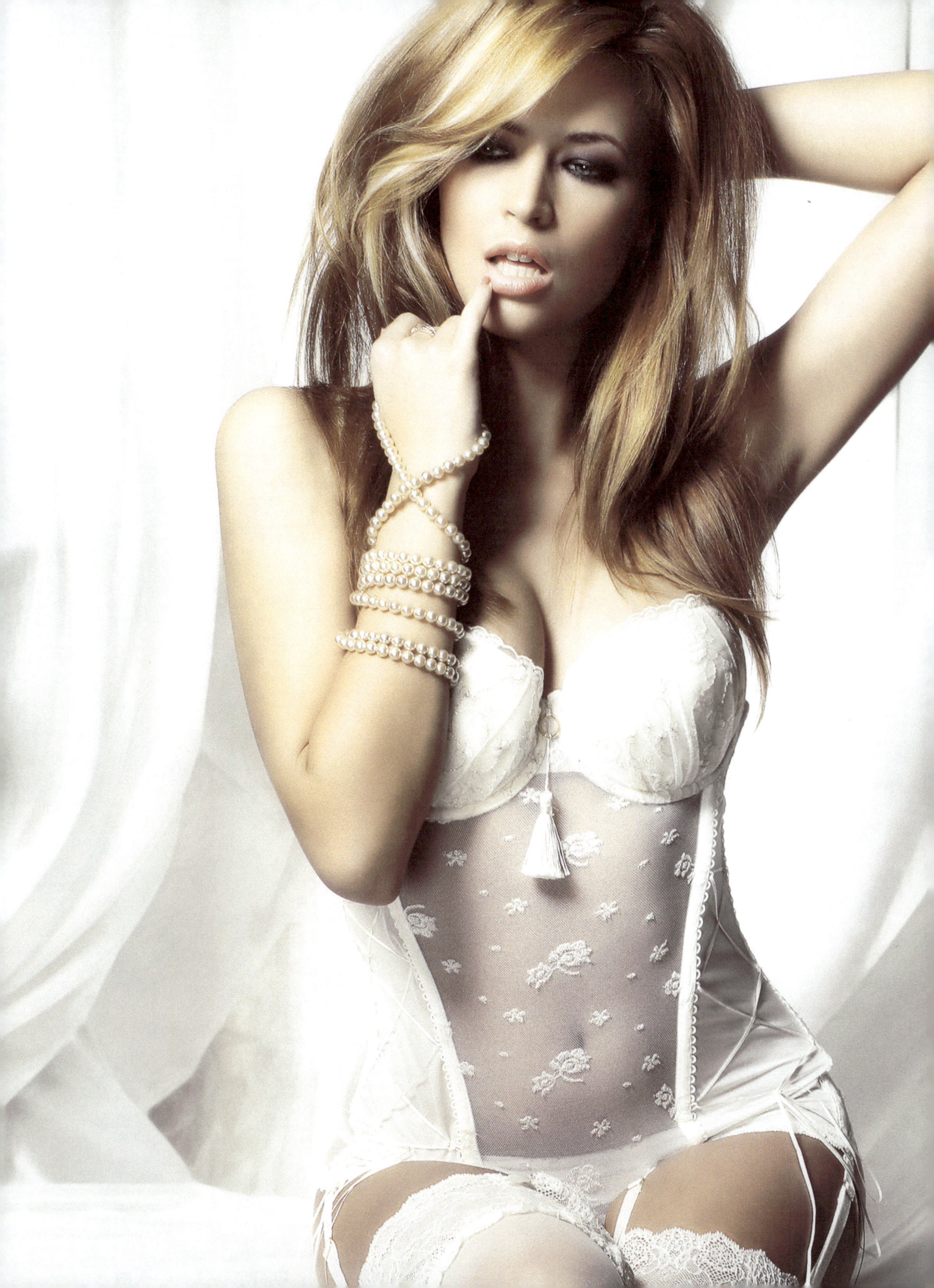

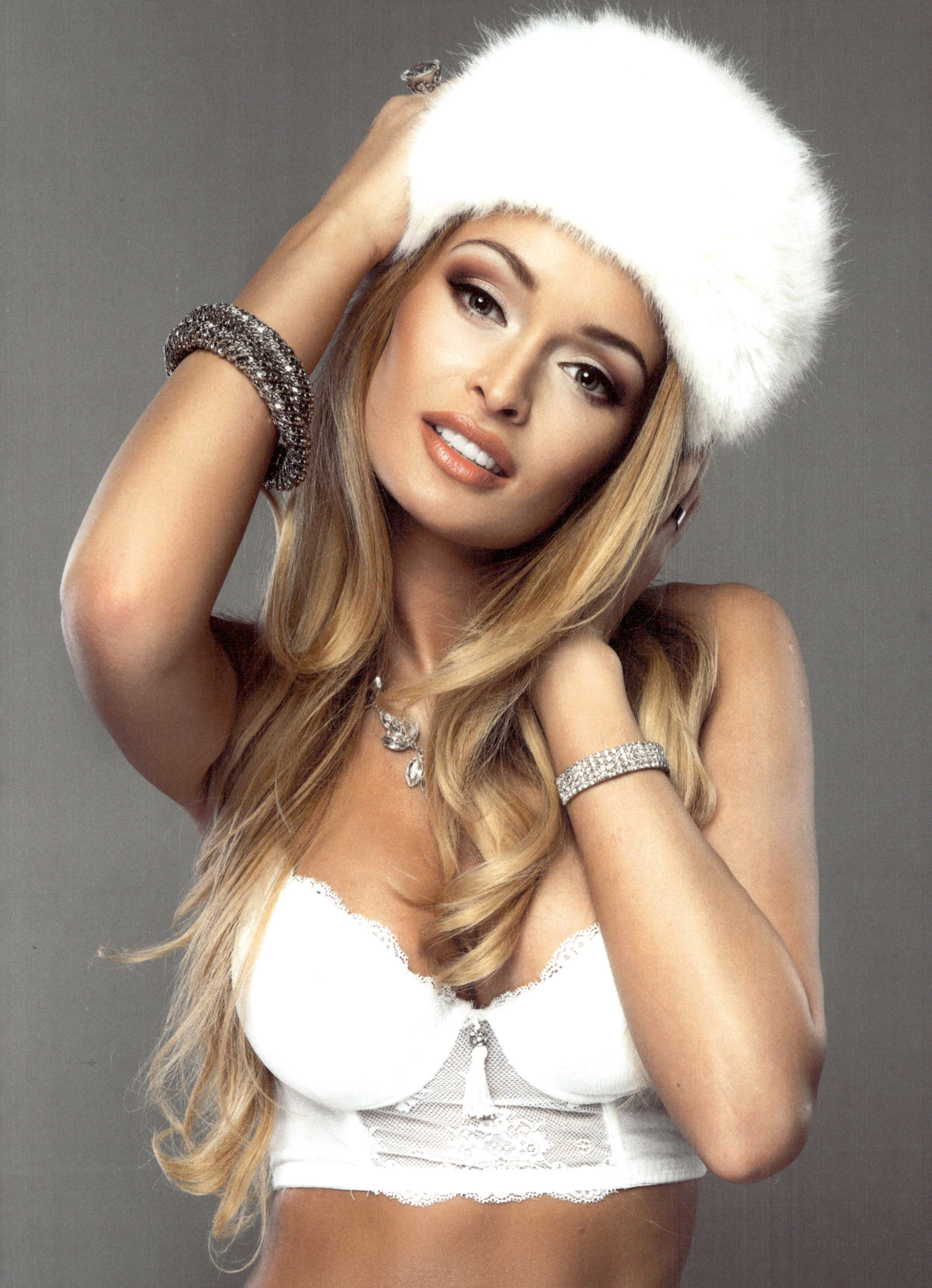

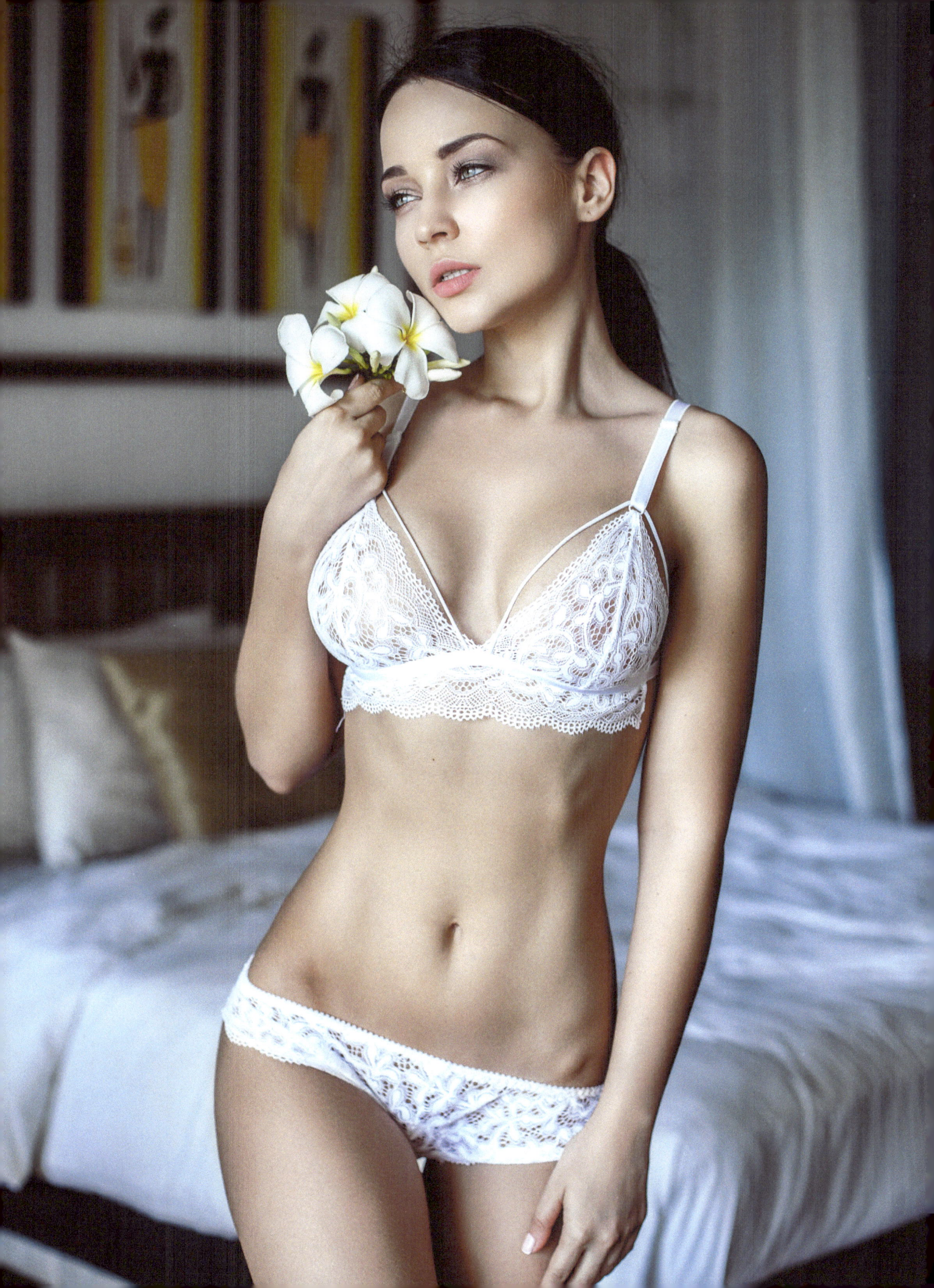

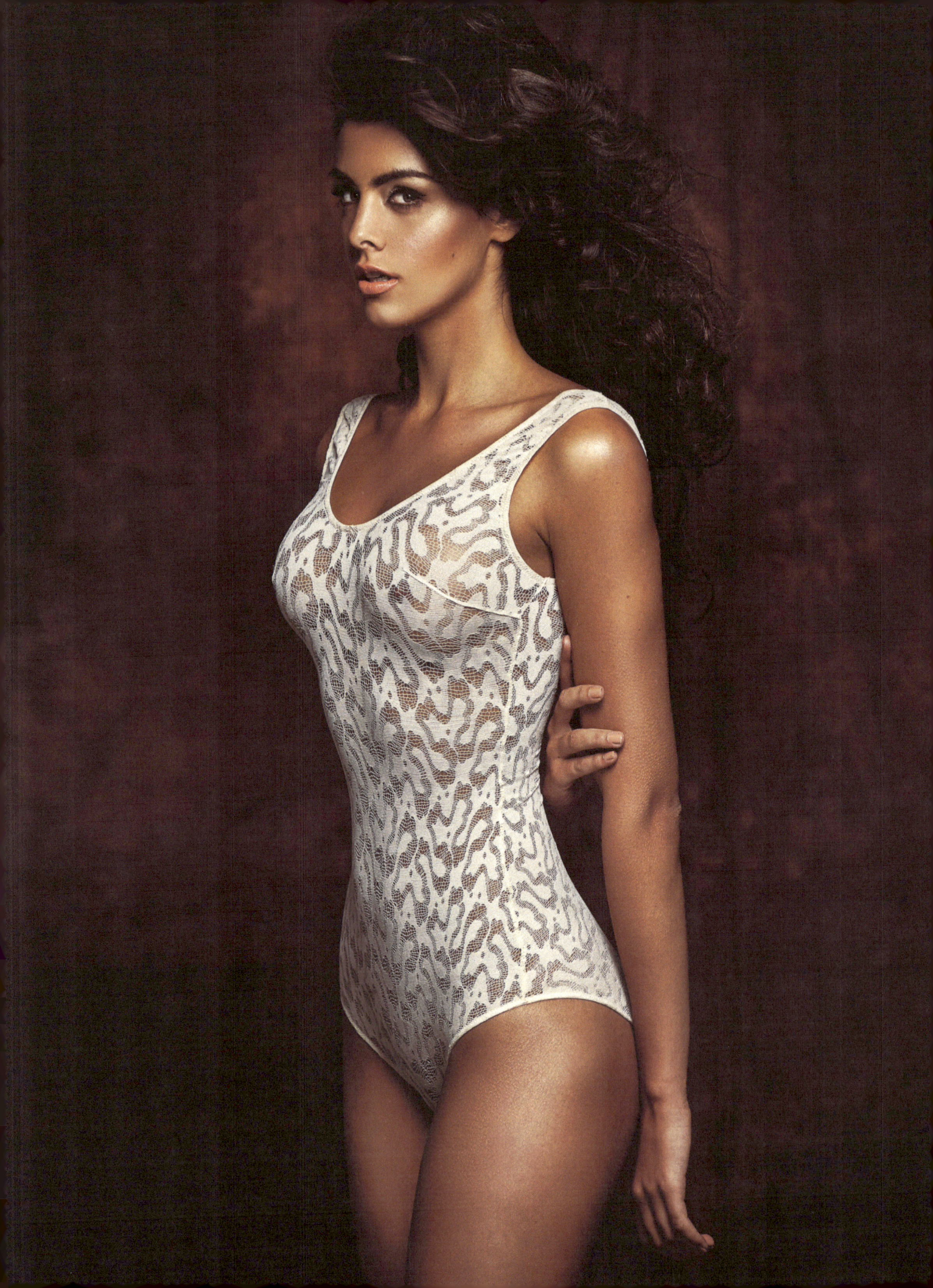

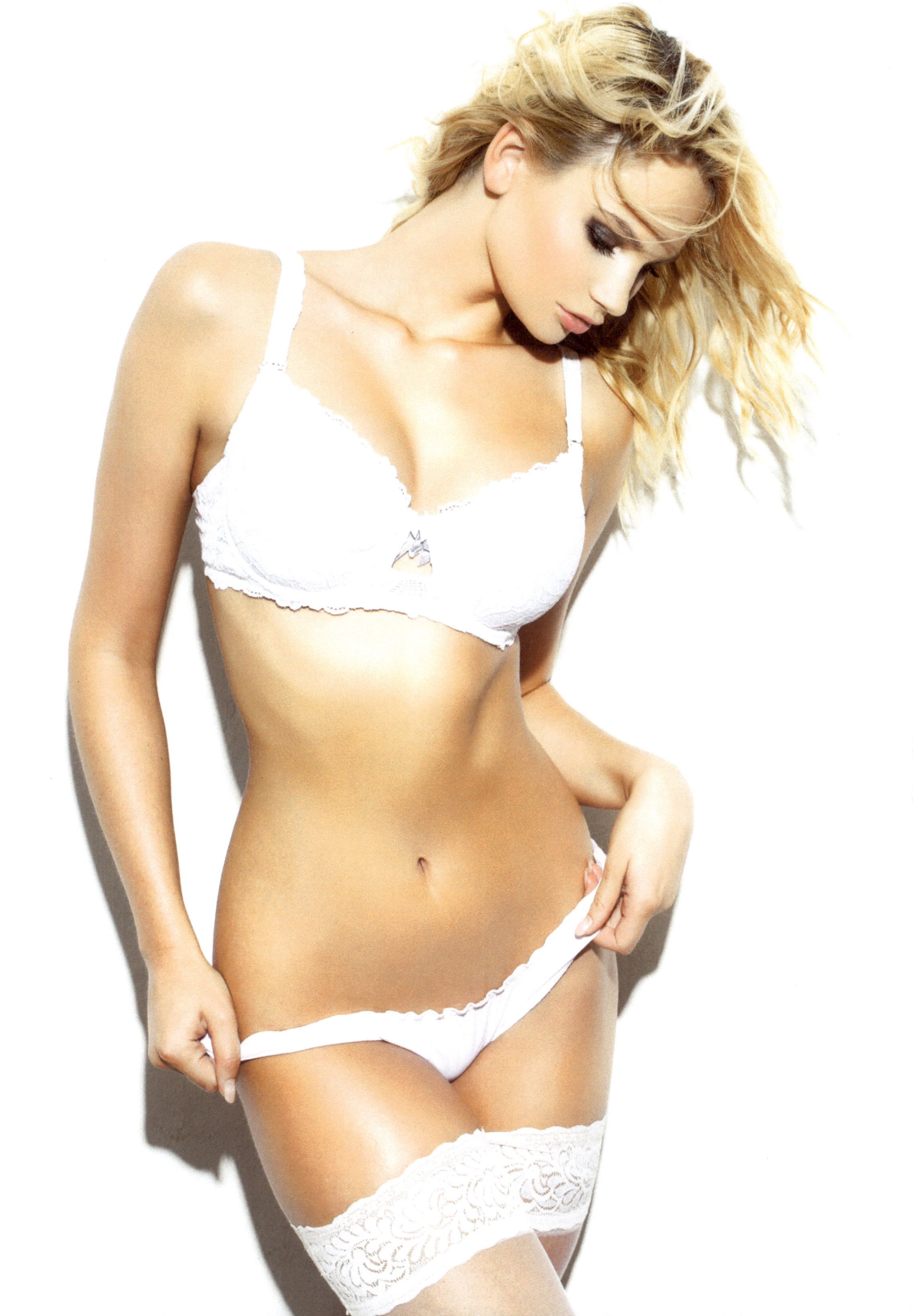

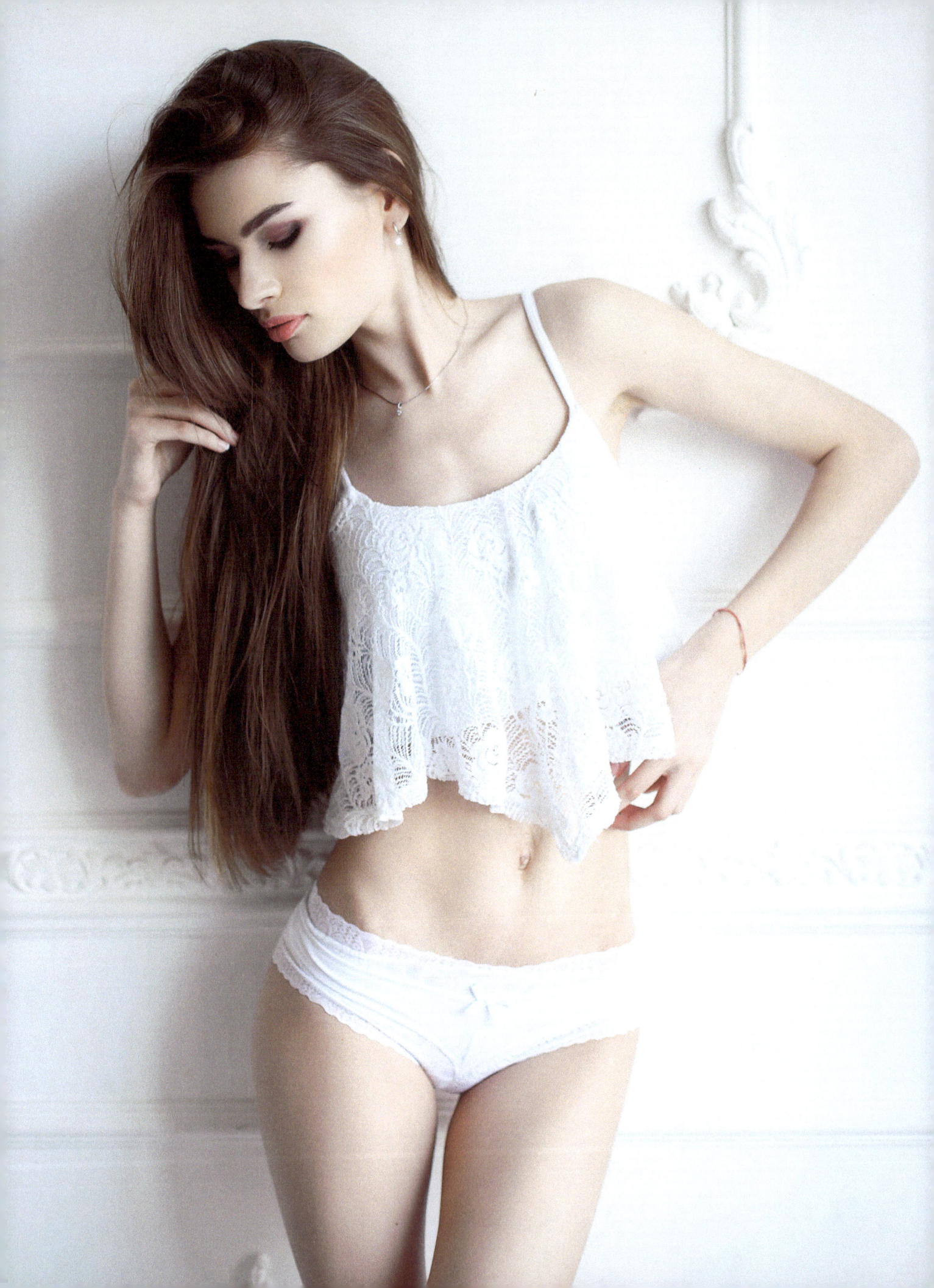

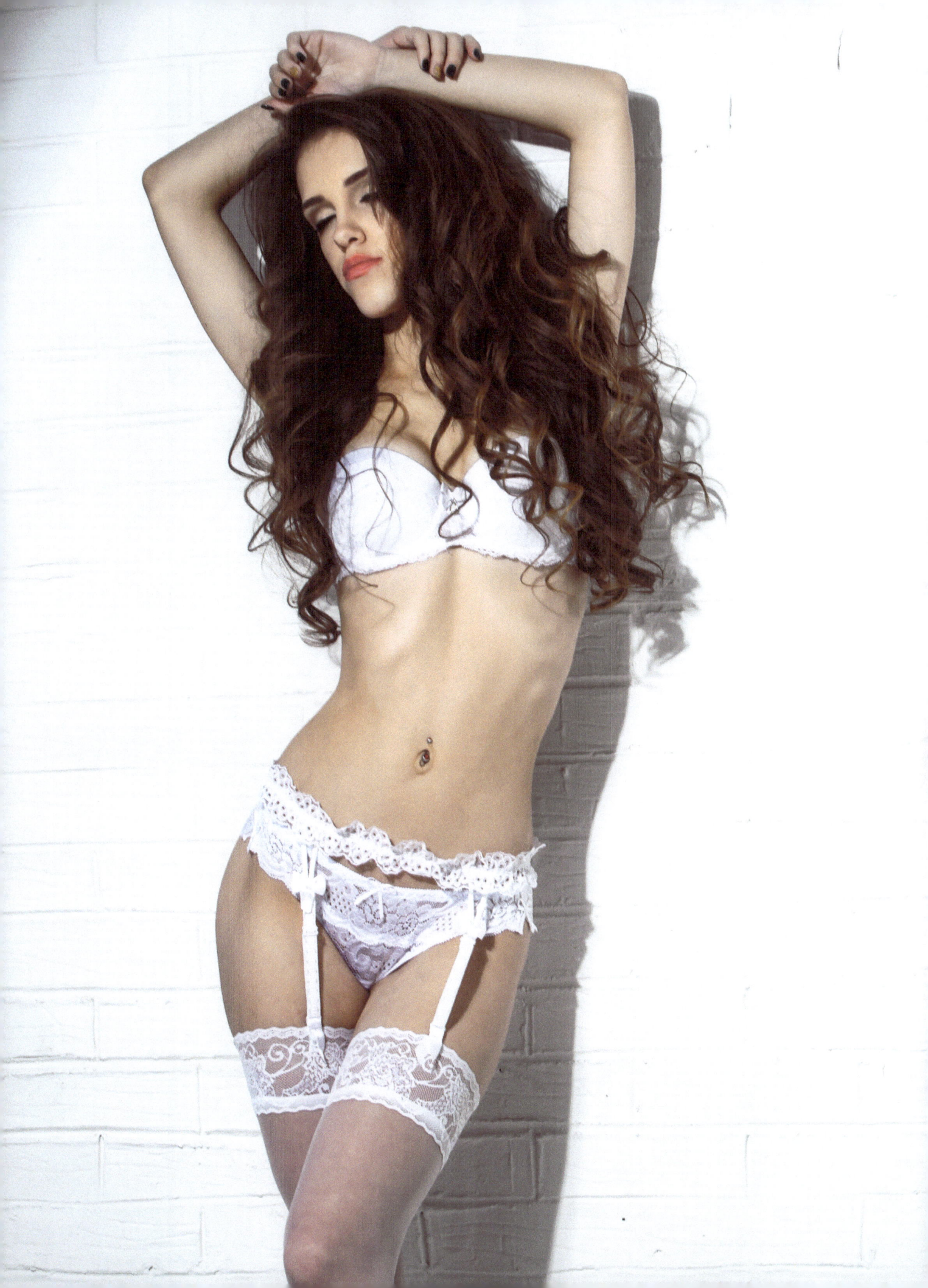

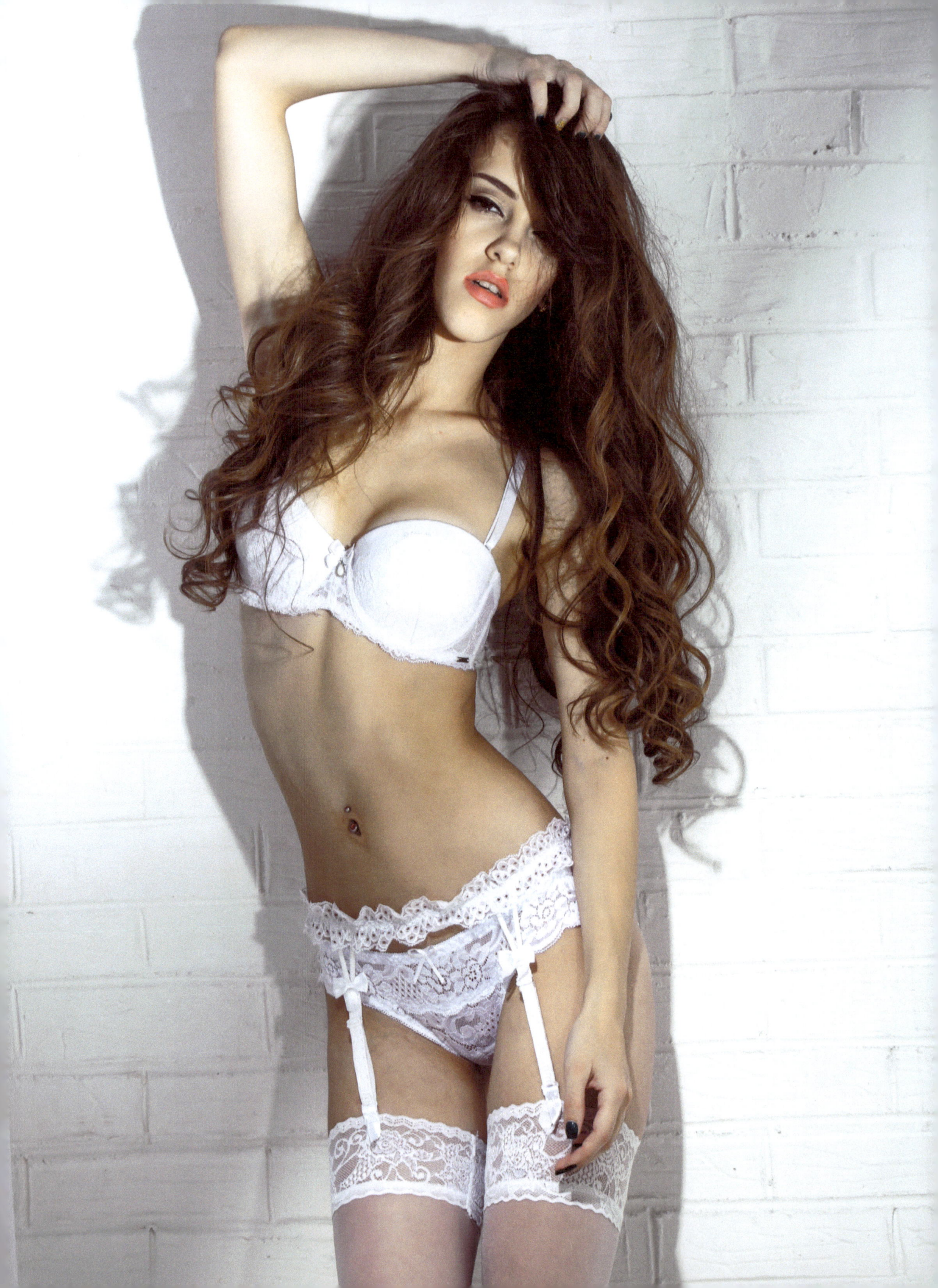

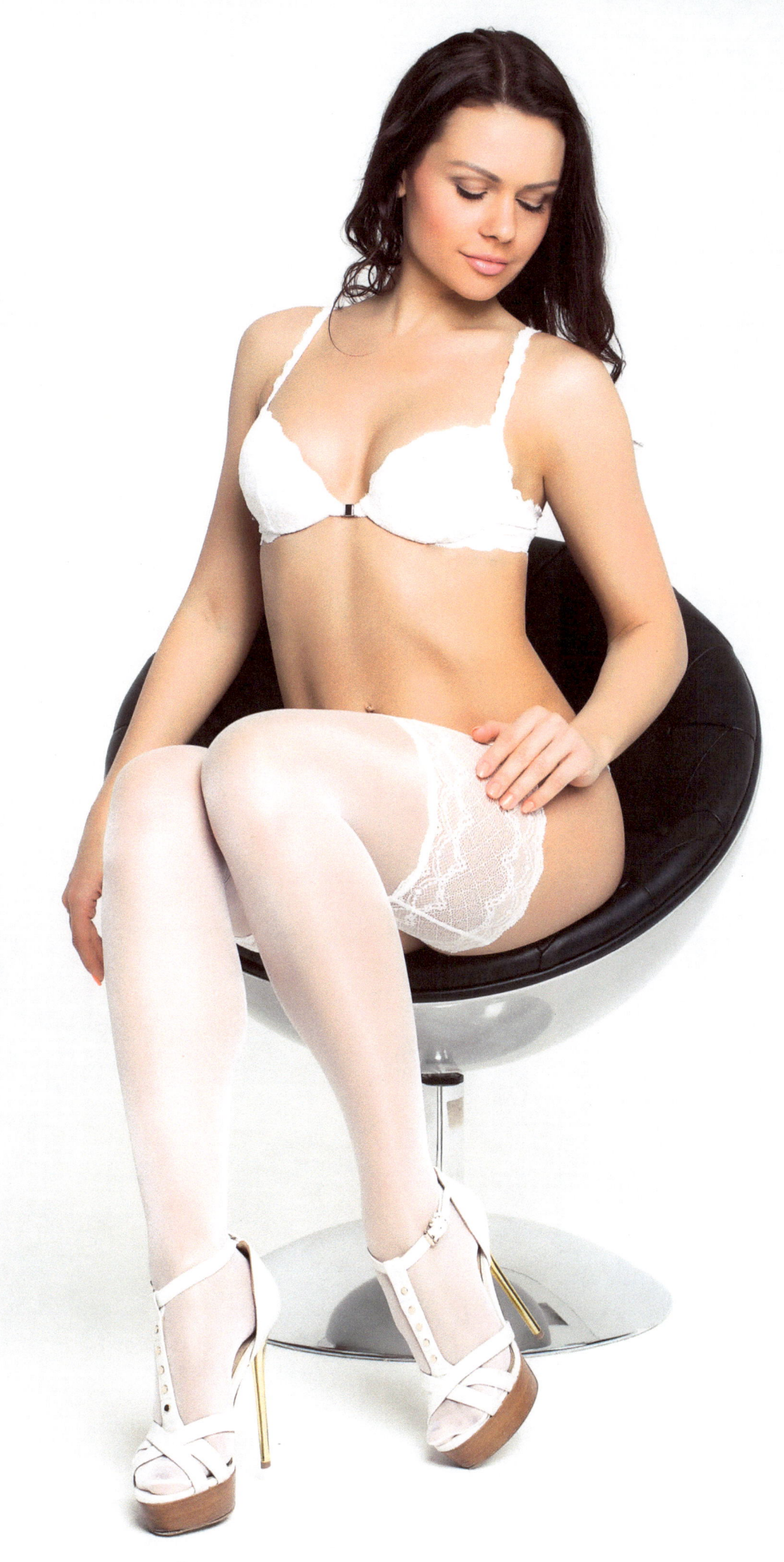

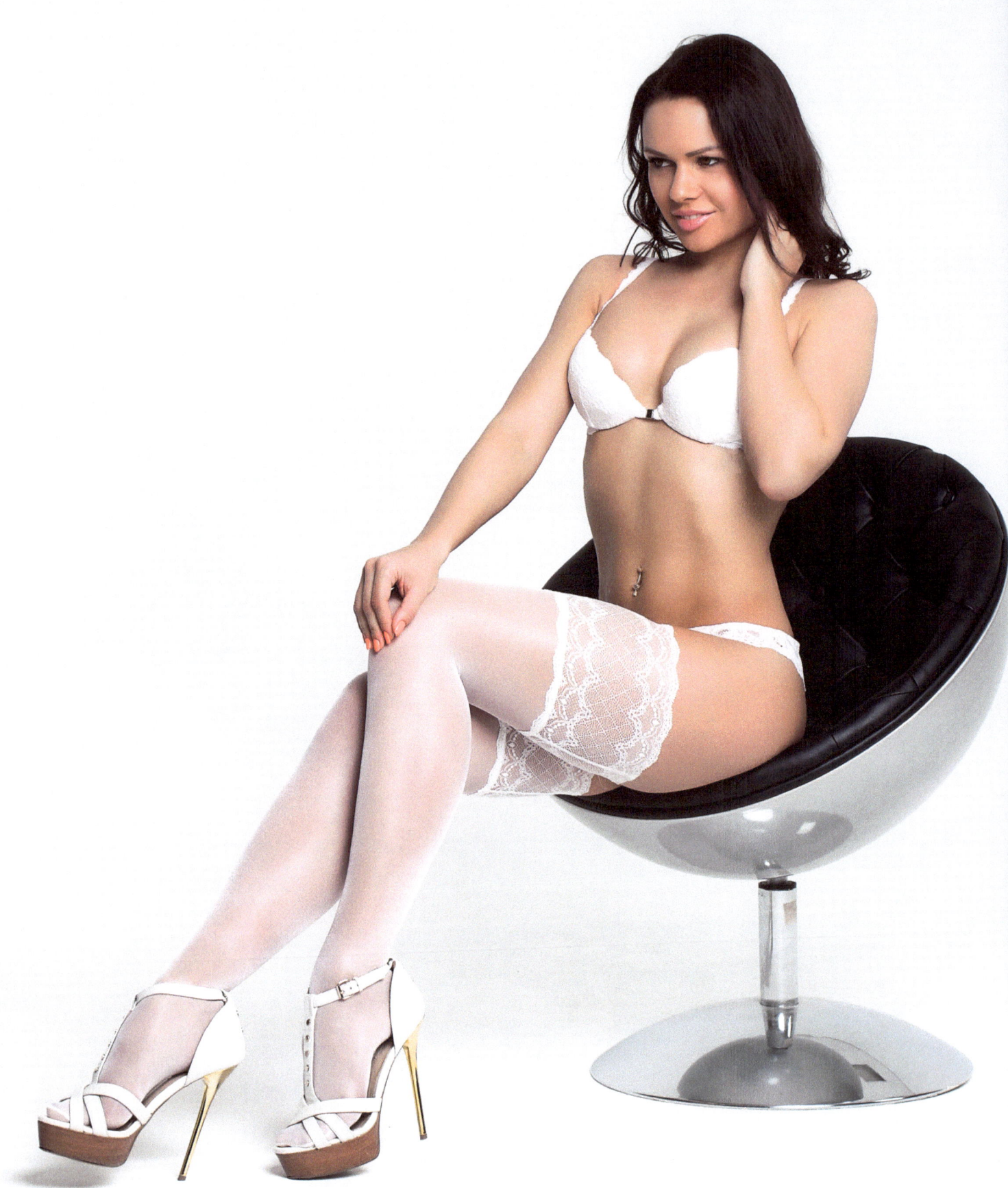

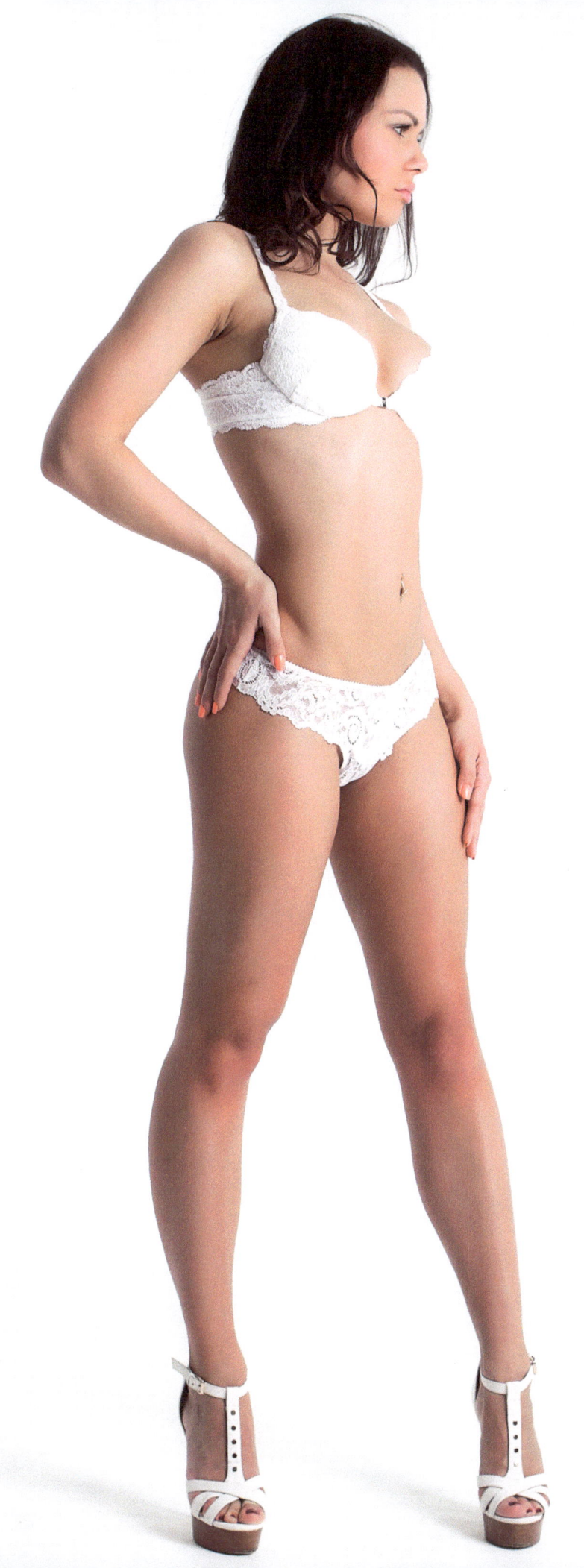